HEARTY
COUNTRY
COOKING

KÖNEMANN

SOUPS

Hearty Pea Soup with Meat

Soup makes an excellent and economical start to a nourishing meal and is especially welcome on a cold day. Some soups, like Hearty Pea Soup with Meat, are substantial enough to be meals in their own right. The recipes here incorporate the best country cooking and characteristic flavours from many countries and are guaranteed to 'warm the cockles of your heart'.
Soup can be prepared in advance and heated up when required. Letting it stand in the refrigerator for a day or two often enhances the flavour.

HINT

For an economical soup, lamb shanks may replace shoulder of lamb. Place shanks in a saucepan, cover with 8 cups of water, bring to the boil, reduce heat and simmer uncovered for 3 hours or until meat falls from the bone. Strain, cool and refrigerate overnight. Skim fat from top of stock. Reserve meat from lamb shanks. Combine stock, vegetables and seasoning. Simmer gently until vegetables are tender, add lamb and serve.

Hearty Pea Soup with Meat

Preparation time:
   Overnight soaking +
   20 minutes
Cooking time:
   1½ hours
Serves 8

1 cup dried green peas
½ cup yellow split peas
6 cups water
3 onions, chopped
500 g potatoes, diced
1 cup sliced carrots
1 cup diced celery
1 kg boned shoulder of
   lamb
1 teaspoon whole
   peppercorns
2 bay leaves
250 g shredded cabbage
chopped parsley

1 Cover peas with cold water and allow to stand overnight.
2 Next day, drain and place in a large saucepan with 6 cups water. Add onions, potatoes, carrots, celery, meat, peppercorns and bay leaves. Cover and cook gently for 1–1½ hours. Skim fat from top. Add shredded cabbage and cook 10 minutes more.
3 Remove meat from soup and cut into slices. Serve either on a plate with the soup or cut pieces smaller and stir into soup. If desired, serve some meat in the soup and maybe serve the remaining meat sliced with mustard or horseradish next day. Sprinkle chopped parsley over soup just before serving.

Vichyssoise

Preparation time:
   10 minutes
Cooking time:
   30 minutes
Serves 4

1 leek
2 tablespoons butter
2 onions, chopped
500 g potatoes, peeled
   and sliced
4 cups vegetable stock
whipped cream
snipped chives

1 Wash and slice leek and cook in butter together with chopped onions until soft, but not brown.
2 Stir in sliced potatoes and stock and cook, covered, until vegetables are tender. Strain and push vegetables through a sieve. Mix well and chill thoroughly. Top with a spoonful of whipped cream and sprinkle with chives just before serving.

Oxtail Soup

Preparation time:
  3 hours
Cooking time:
  1 hour
Serves 8

1 kg oxtail, jointed
10 cups water
plain flour
pepper
30 g butter
125 g bacon pieces, with
  excess fat removed
2 onions, sliced
3 carrots, sliced
¾ cup chopped celery
2 parsley sprigs
1 bay leaf
1 thyme sprig
12 peppercorns
3 tablespoons barley
chopped parsley

1 Put oxtail in a saucepan with water. Bring to the boil and simmer gently for about 2 hours. Remove oxtail and pat dry. Chill the stock. Coat oxtail with flour seasoned with pepper.
2 Melt butter and slowly fry oxtail until browned. Add bacon, onions, carrots and celery and cook over gentle heat until the vegetables are browned. Remove solid fat from stock and pour stock over oxtail and vegetables. Add parsley, bay leaf and thyme, tied together, and the peppercorns. Slowly bring to the boil. Skim the surface, cover, and simmer for 1 hour.
3 Lift oxtail pieces from pan. Wash barley and add to pan. Remove oxtail flesh from bones and return to pan. Cover and simmer for 1 hour. Remove bunch of herbs. Serve sprinkled with chopped parsley.

HINT
Canned tomato purée or tomato paste may be added with the barley for a flavour boost. Use 1 cup of tomato purée or ¼ cup tomato paste.

French Onion Soup

Preparation time:
  20 minutes
Cooking time:
  45 minutes
Serves 4

500 g onions
60 g butter
2 vegetable or beef stock
  cubes
5 cups water
1 leek, sliced
pinch dried thyme
2 cloves garlic, crushed
freshly ground black
  pepper
¼ cup dry white wine
sliced French bread
250 g Gruyère or
  Emmenthal cheese,
  grated

1 Peel onions and slice thinly. Cook very slowly over a low heat in butter until soft and golden. Stir in stock cubes, water, leek, thyme, garlic, and pepper.
2 Simmer, covered, for 25–30 minutes. Stir in wine.
3 Pour into a large ovenproof bowl or into individual heatproof bowls. Cover with bread slices and grated cheese.
4 Bake in a hot oven 240°C (200°C gas) until cheese bubbles and is golden brown.

Note. The secret to a flavoursome French onion soup is the browning of the onions. Cook onions over a very low heat, stirring until golden brown. This can take up to 20 minutes.

HINT
French bread may be brushed with extra butter and crushed garlic, toasted until crisp and then sprinkled with cheese before adding to the soup bowls.

French Onion Soup

Mulligatawny

Return to soup with lemon juice and cream; gently reheat.

4 Serve in heated bowls, with hot boiled rice and chutney offered separately to stir into the soup. You might also like to offer other accompaniments such as coconut, sultanas, or chopped peanuts.

Borsch

Preparation time:
  1 hour
Cooking time:
  15 minutes
Serves 8

1 kg shin of beef
8 cups water
1 onion, chopped
3 bay leaves
1 teaspoon whole
  allspice
2 tomatoes, peeled and
  chopped
2 potatoes, peeled, cut
  into thin strips
2 carrots, peeled, cut
  into thin strips
1 small cabbage,
  shredded
750 g beetroot, cut into
  thin strips
2 teaspoons vinegar
freshly ground pepper
¼ cup chopped parsley
2 tablespoons snipped
  fresh dill

1 Put beef, water,

Mulligatawny

Preparation time:
  30 minutes
Cooking time:
  1 hour
Serves 6

1 kg chicken pieces, such
  as thighs, drumsticks,
  breasts
2 tablespoons plain flour
2 teaspoons curry
  powder
1 teaspoon turmeric
½ teaspoon ground
  ginger
60 g butter
6 cloves
12 peppercorns
1 large apple, peeled and
  diced
6 cups chicken stock

2 tablespoons lemon
  juice
½ cup fresh cream
boiled rice and chutney
  to serve

1 Wipe chicken pieces with paper towels. Combine flour, curry powder, turmeric and ginger and rub well into chicken.
2 Heat butter in a heavy saucepan and lightly brown the chicken on all sides. Add cloves, peppercorns, apple and stock, bring to the boil, and simmer covered for 1 hour.
3 Remove chicken pieces and discard peppercorns and cloves. Skin chicken and cut flesh into small dice.

onion, bay leaves and allspice into a large saucepan and bring to boil. Skim if necessary and cook with lid on for 1 hour or until tender.

2 While meat is cooking collect all the vegetables together. It is best to be patient and use a sharp knife to cut vegetables rather than grate them. If they are grated the soup will be cloudy. When meat is cooked remove from pot. Cut into thick strips from the bone and return meat to the pot. Add all the vegetables and allow to boil without the lid on for about 15 minutes. If you cook with the lid on, the soup will not retain its bright attractive colour.

3 Stir in vinegar, pepper, parsley and dill. Serve piping hot with black bread and a spoonful of whipped cream flavoured with horseradish cream.

HINT

Do not discard the leaves from young beetroot. Fresh raw leaves are delicious in tossed salads, or shredded and cooked with garlic and butter.

Borsch

Greek Chicken Soup

Preparation time:
  1 hour plus overnight chilling
Cooking time:
  20 minutes
Serves 6

1 x 1 kg chicken
6 cups water
1 carrot sliced
1 onion sliced
1 stalk celery, sliced
1 teaspoon fresh thyme
1 bay leaf
2 garlic cloves, chopped
1 teaspoon whole white
  peppercorns
¼ cup rice
pepper
1 tablespoon vegetable
  oil
1 egg yolk
2 eggs
juice 1 lemon
snipped chives

1 Place chicken, water, carrot, onion, celery, thyme, bay leaf, garlic and peppercorns in saucepan. Bring to boil, skim if necessary and cook until chicken is tender. Remove chicken from stock; cool. Cut into small pieces. Strain stock; chill.
2 Remove fat from top of stock. Sauté rice in hot oil for a few minutes, add to chicken stock and cook for 15 minutes until rice is cooked. Stir in chicken.

Taste for seasoning and add pepper if necessary. If a more filling soup is desired, double the amount of rice.
3 Beat egg yolk, eggs and lemon juice together and carefully beat into this a little of the hot soup. Add this to the rest of the hot soup, stirring all the time. Do not allow to boil, but reheat only, otherwise the soup will curdle.
4 Serve immediately with bread and cheese. Sprinkle snipped chives over top.

Seafood Soup

Preparation time:
  15 minutes
Cooking time:
  15 minutes
Serves 4

1 leek
1 fennel bulb
½ cup sliced celery
8 mushrooms, sliced
1 clove garlic, crushed
3 tablespoons olive oil
4 cups fish stock
1 bay leaf
2 teaspoons lemon juice
pepper
500 g gemfish, diced
125 g scallops
250 g green prawns,
  shelled
¼ cup dry white wine
½ cup mayonnaise
3 cloves garlic, crushed
croûtons

1 Wash leek and cut into strips together with fennel bulb. Add celery, mushrooms and garlic, and cook in hot oil for 10 minutes. Stir in fish stock, bay leaf, lemon juice and pepper to taste. Simmer for 5 minutes.
2 Add diced fish and scallops and cook gently for 5 minutes. Stir in prawns and wine. Taste to see if more seasoning is needed. Reheat gently.
3 Mix mayonnaise and garlic together; if too thick stir in some milk. Serve soup in bowls with croûtons and spoon on a little of the mayonnaise mixture.

Provençal Vegetable Soup

Preparation time:
 15 minutes
Cooking time:
 40 minutes
Serves 6

6 cups water
1 cup diced potato
1 cup diced carrot
1 large leek, cut into
 strips
1 cup sliced green beans
1 x 310 g can butter
 beans
½ cup broken pieces
 spaghetti

½ cup soft breadcrumbs
2 cloves garlic
2 tablespoons tomato
 paste
2 tablespoons fresh basil
 leaves
¼ cup grated Parmesan
 cheese
1 teaspoon curry paste
2 tablespoons olive oil

1 Pour water into a large saucepan. Add potato, carrot, leek and green beans. Cook for 20 minutes with lid on.
2 Add butter beans, spaghetti and breadcrumbs and cook uncovered for another 12 minutes or until spaghetti is tender.

3 Blend garlic, tomato paste, basil, Parmesan and curry paste in a blender. Add olive oil a few drops at a time. If desired these ingredients may be worked to a paste with a pestle and mortar. Stir into hot soup and serve with extra grated Parmesan and crusty bread.

Provencal Vegetable Soup, Seafood Soup and Greek Chicken Soup

9

SEAFOOD

Trout Almondine

*F*ish and shellfish make a pleasant change from meat either as a delightful meal or a tempting first course. Fish is an easily digested food to tempt the most finicky appetite, perhaps gently cooked in butter or creamed and baked in a feather-light vol-au-vent. As fish does not require cooking for long, these recipes are all quick and easy.

Trout Almondine

Preparation time:
   10 minutes
Cooking time:
   12 minutes
Serves 4

4 medium trout
plain flour
pepper
125 g butter
2 teaspoons lemon juice
freshly ground pepper
⅓ cup blanched
   almonds, toasted and
   split into halves
lemon wedges

1 Trim fins of each trout close to body, leaving head and tail intact. Toss in flour seasoned with pepper.
2 Melt half the butter in a frying pan. Add fish and cook until browned underneath. Turn and brown the other side.
3 Carefully lift fish on

to a heated serving platter and keep warm. Add the rest of the butter to the pan with lemon juice, pepper, and almonds. Cook, stirring, for 2–3 minutes. Pour over fish and serve at once with the lemon wedges.

HINT
Trout has small scales, soft skin and soft flesh with a mild flavour. When scaling the fish be careful not to tear the skin. Trout is usually served whole.

Baked Fish with Herb Stuffing

Preparation time:
   20 minutes
Cooking time:
   45 minutes
Serves 4

1 large snapper or other
   whole fish
125 g butter
2 cups bread cubes
4 rashers of bacon,
   chopped
1 small clove garlic,
   crushed
1 stick celery, sliced

3 shallots, finely
   chopped
1 tablespoon chopped
   fresh thyme
freshly ground pepper
a little melted butter
sliced limes or lemons to
   garnish

1 Wipe cavity of fish and place fish on an oiled baking dish. Heat butter in a large pan, add bread cubes and fry until crisp and golden. Remove from pan and set aside to cool.
2 Place bacon in the same pan, and fry until crisp. Add garlic, celery and shallots and cook until soft, about 5 minutes. Combine with bread cubes, herbs and pepper.
3 Spoon filling into fish and brush fish with melted butter. Bake in a preheated moderate oven (180°C) for about 45 minutes, or until flesh is white and opaque and flakes easily when tested with a fork. To serve, cut fish into slices and serve each with a spoonful of herbed bread stuffing. Garnish with lime or lemon slices.

HINT
When buying whole fish look for clear, bulging eyes, shining skin and close-fitting scales.

Fish Parisienne

Preparation time:
  15 minutes
Cooking time:
  25 minutes
Serves 4

500 g firm-fleshed fish
  fillets
1 ³/4 cups water
1 small celery stalk
¹/2 small onion
2 parsley sprigs
1 bay leaf
²/3 cup dry white wine
125 g shallots, split into
  halves
250 g green prawns,
  shelled and deveined
185 g small mushrooms,
  thinly sliced
3 shallots, finely
  chopped
35 g butter
pepper
1 tablespoon plain flour
buttered breadcrumbs

1 Remove skin from
fish and cut flesh into
small cubes, taking out
bones. Heat water with
celery, onion, parsley,
bay leaf, and wine until
boiling. Simmer for 5
minutes. Add fish and
simmer until just tender.
Remove fish with a
slotted spoon and put
aside. Add scallops
and prawns to pan and
simmer for 2 minutes.
Remove scallops and
prawns. Strain the liquid
and reserve 1¹/4 cups.
2 Cook mushrooms and
shallots gently in 15 g
butter until softened.
Add pepper to taste.
Spoon into 4 shell-
shaped individual
ovenproof dishes, or into
a shallow ovenproof dish.
3 Melt remaining 20 g
butter, add flour, and stir
for a minute. Gradually
add reserved fish stock
and cook, stirring until
boiling. Simmer for 3-4
minutes. Add pepper,
then the fish, prawns
and scallops. Simmer for
2 minutes to reheat.
4 Spoon into the dishes
or dish. Top with
buttered crumbs (about
6 tablespoons tossed in
3 tablespoons of melted
butter over medium heat
until crisp). Serve
immediately.

HINT
Enrich Fish
Parisienne by
substituting ¼ cup
cream for ¼ cup fish
stock.

HINT
Fresh ginger may be
peeled and stored
covered with sherry
in a screw-top jar for
up to 6 months in the
refrigerator.

Mr Lee's Stir-Fry

Preparation time:
  15 minutes
Cooking time:
  5 minutes
Serves 2

1 tablespoon vegetable
  oil
1 clove garlic, crushed
2 Chinese cabbage
  leaves, sliced
1 carrot, cut in thin
  strips
1 small turnip, cut in
  thin strips
1 white onion, sliced
  lengthways
4 mushrooms, sliced
2 teaspoons chopped
  fresh coriander
1 teaspoon finely
  chopped fresh ginger
1 tablespoon honey
1 tablespoon lemon juice
12 green yabbies or 6
  prawns, shelled
1 tablespoon soy sauce

1 Heat oil in a large
heavy frying pan or
wok. Add garlic. Stir-fry
cabbage, carrot, turnip,
onion and mushrooms
until lightly cooked.
2 Add coriander,
ginger, honey and lemon
juice and toss quickly to
blend flavours. Add
yabbies or prawns and
soy sauce and toss
quickly to heat. Serve
with steamed rice or
noodles.

Mr Lee's Stir-Fry

Shellfish Vol-Au-Vent

Shellfish Vol-au-vent

Preparation time:
    30 minutes
Cooking time:
    10 minutes
Serves 4

3 tablespoons butter
1 small leek, thinly sliced
125 g mushrooms,
    thinly sliced
3 tablespoons flour
1½ cups milk
¼ cup white wine
¼ cup cream
1 egg yolk
½ teaspoon tarragon
pepper
1 dozen oysters, shelled
1 dozen mussels, shelled
18 or 20 cm vol-au-vent
    case
chopped parsley
1 shallot, finely chopped
paprika

1 Melt butter, add leek
and mushrooms and
cook gently until just
softened. Sprinkle in
flour, stir a few minutes
and slowly add milk.
Cook, stirring until
thickened. Stir in wine
and cook over low heat
a few more minutes.
Remove from heat.
2 Beat cream lightly
with egg yolk and stir
slowly into sauce. Add
tarragon and season
with pepper. Add
oysters and mussels, and
simmer gently for 2–3
minutes.

3 Meanwhile, heat
through the pastry case
in a moderate oven.
Spoon shellfish mixture
into the case and garnish
with parsley, shallot and
a dusting of paprika.
Serve at once.

HINT
Vol-au-vent cases are
readily available in
supermarkets and
some bakeries. If the
large vol-au-vent case
is unavailable, use
individual cases.

Creamed Mussels

Preparation time:
    15 minutes
Cooking time:
    15 minutes
Serves 4

36 fresh mussels
water to cover
60 g butter
2 tablespoons plain flour
1½ cups cooking liquid
    from mussels
1 clove garlic, crushed
⅓ cup dry white wine
2 egg yolks
2 tablespoons lemon
    juice
⅓ cup cream
freshly ground pepper

*finely chopped parsley to
    garnish*

1 Wash mussels in cold
running water and scrub
with a stiff brush until
clean. Discard any that
are not tightly closed.
Place in a wide sauce-
pan, cover with boiling
water, and boil rapidly
for 5 minutes, or until
they open. Discard any
that do not open.
Remove mussels from
their shells, reserving the
best shells for serving the
mussels. Strain the
cooking liquid and save
1½ cups.
2 Melt butter, stir in
flour over low heat, and
cook for 1 minute.
Remove from heat and
stir in warm cooking
liquid and garlic. Bring
to the boil and simmer
for 5 minutes.
3 Whisk wine, egg
yolks, lemon juice and
cream together and stir
into pan. Continue
stirring until sauce
thickens, and season to
taste with pepper.
Return mussels to pan
and gently reheat.
4 Spoon into shells and
sprinkle with chopped
parsley.

HINT
Mussels are often
called the poor man's
oyster. Take care not
to overcook as they
toughen easily.

Tuna Chowder

Preparation time:
  20 minutes
Cooking time:
  15 minutes
Serves 4

250 g potatoes, peeled
  and diced
15 g butter
2 bacon rashers, cut into
  small squares, with
  rind removed
2 medium onions, thinly
  sliced
1 x 375 mL can
  evaporated milk
pepper
1 x 425 g can tuna
chopped parsley

1 Cook potatoes in 2
cups of boiling water for
about 8 minutes.
Remove pan from heat.
2 Melt butter and gently
fry bacon and onions
until onions are
transparent and bacon is
crisp. Add to potatoes in
saucepan.
3 Gradually stir in
evaporated milk and
season with pepper.
Simmer for 10 minutes.
4 Drain and flake tuna,
add to pan, and simmer
for 5–7 minutes, or until
heated through. Sprinkle
with chopped parsley.

Sailors' Pie

Preparation time:
  20 minutes
Cooking time:
  20 minutes
Serves 4

1 kg potatoes
1 x 56 g can flat anchovy
  fillets, drained
¼ cup grated tasty
  cheese
¼ cup chopped parsley
½ cup sour cream
375 g white
  firm-fleshed fish
pepper
250 g scallops or mussels

1 Peel potatoes and
cook in boiling water
until tender. Drain.
Chop anchovies and mix
with cheese, parsley and
sour cream.
2 Place fish fillets on
one half of a greased
ovenproof dish. Season
with pepper to taste and
add scallops or mussels.
Cover with anchovy
mixture.
3 Press potatoes
through a sieve directly
into the remaining half
of the dish, next to fish.
Bake in a moderate
oven (180°C) for
20–25 minutes until
fish flakes when tested
with a fork and top is
lightly browned.

Sailors' Pie

Barbecued Fish in Foil

Preparation time:
   15 minutes
Cooking time:
   40 minutes
Serves 4

1 kg snapper, bream or
   jewfish
garlic salt
20 g butter, melted
lemon pepper
1 tablespoon butter
2 tablespoons chopped
   shallots
3/4 cup chopped
   mushrooms
2 tablespoons chopped
   parsley
1 lemon

1 Make three diagonal incisions about 2.5 cm apart on each side of fish, in the thickest part. Sprinkle inside of fish with garlic salt and lemon pepper.
2 Melt 1 tablespoon butter and gently fry shallots and chopped mushrooms until softened. Stir in parsley. Spoon mixture into cavity of fish and add two or three slices of lemon. Secure opening with small skewers.
3 Lightly butter a piece of heavy foil large enough to enclose the fish. Put fish in centre and squeeze over juice from rest of lemon. Bring edges of foil up and fold loosely over fish enclosing it completely. Cook in a moderate oven (180°C) for about 40 minutes or barbecue until tender when tested with a fork.

HINT
Whole fish are scored with diagonal cuts across the thickest part of body for even cooking.

Coromandel Prawns

Preparation time:
   20 minutes
Cooking time:
   20 minutes
Serves 4

60 g butter
2 teaspoons curry
   powder
4 shallots, sliced
1 clove garlic, crushed
1 capsicum, sliced
3/4 cup evaporated milk
1 tablespoon tomato
   paste
2 teaspoons soy sauce
1/2 cup sour cream
1 tablespoon dry sherry
750 g prawns, shelled
1 x 250 g packet frozen
   spinach, thawed

1 Melt butter, add curry powder, shallots, garlic and capsicum and cook for a few minutes until softened. Stir in evaporated milk, tomato paste and soy sauce and cook gently for 3 to 4 minutes.
2 Add sour cream, sherry and prawns and stir until evenly mixed and hot. Do not cook any longer at this stage.
3 Press water out of spinach and cook until tender. Drain, place on serving dish and top with the curried prawns. Serve with rice and lots of crusty bread.

HINT
Fresh green or frozen prawns may be used in this recipe.

HINT
Spice should be bought in small quantities, and stored in airtight containers in a cool dark place.

Coromandel Prawns

MEAT AND POULTRY

Chicken Provençal

These meat and chicken recipes from the country were created for people like settlers and shearers doing hard physical work all day. Even in our mainly urban society good sustaining food is still needed, especially for growing children, and these dishes are just the thing for a hungry family. Savoury casseroles and stews make good use of the cheaper cuts of meat and the recipes that follow provide the ideas for interesting combinations of ingredients and flavourings.

Chicken Provençal

Preparation time:
   15 minutes
Cooking time:
   40 minutes
Serves 4

2 tablespoons oil
30 g butter
1.5 kg chicken pieces
2 tablespoons brandy
¾ cup dry white wine
4 tomatoes, peeled
8 small onions, peeled
1 apple, peeled and
   diced
½ cup green olives
1 teaspoon curry powder
½ teaspoon dried thyme
250 g button
   mushrooms
chopped parsley
snipped chives

1 Heat oil and butter together. Add chicken pieces and brown all over. Pour off remaining oil and butter and reserve for cooking the mushrooms.
2 Pour brandy over chicken. Add wine, tomatoes, onions, apple, olives, curry powder and thyme. Cover with a tight-fitting lid and cook gently until tender, about 30–35 minutes, adding a little extra wine if necessary.
3 Cook mushrooms in reserved oil and butter, add to chicken and sprinkle top with parsley and chives. Serve with ribbon noodles.

HINT
To peel tomatoes make a small cross with a sharp knife and dip in boiling water for a minute or two; skin will peel off easily.

Italian Lemon Chicken

Preparation time:
   10 minutes
Cooking time:
   40 minutes
Serves 4

1.5 kg small chicken
   pieces
pepper
½ teaspoon dried
   rosemary
2 tablespoons vegetable
   oil
1 clove garlic, crushed
½ cup dry white wine
2 eggs
2 tablespoons lemon
   juice
1 tablespoon finely
   chopped parsley

1 Sprinkle chicken pieces with pepper and rosemary. Heat oil and brown chicken on both sides. Cook until tender.
2 Stir in garlic and wine, remove chicken from pan and place on serving plate. Beat eggs with lemon juice and pour into pan, stirring all the time. The egg must not be allowed to cook, just to thicken. Pour over chicken and sprinkle with parsley. Serve at once with buttered noodles and a green salad.

Picnic Egg and Chicken Pie

Picnic Egg and Chicken Pie

Preparation time:
  40 minutes
Cooking time:
  1½ hours
Serves 8

1 cup plain flour
1 cup self-raising flour
150 g butter, chopped
1 egg yolk, lightly beaten
cold water
8 chicken breasts

1 ham steak
6 spring onions, finely
  chopped
1 tablespoon chopped
  parsley
1 teaspoon mixed dried
  herbs
pepper
5 hard-boiled eggs
beaten egg yolk for
  glazing

1 Sift flours into a mixing bowl. Rub butter in with fingertips until mixture resembles breadcrumbs. Add egg

yolk with enough cold water to form a firm dough. Chill for about 30 minutes.
2 Take two-thirds and roll out to fit into a 23 cm greased spring-form tin. Shred chicken breasts and cube ham steak. In a bowl, mix with spring onions, parsley, mixed herbs and pepper.
3 Spread half of the mixture into pastry case. Arrange the whole shelled hard-boiled eggs

over the top and cover with the remaining mixture. Roll out rest of pastry to form a cover. Moisten the edges of pastry case and place cover on top, pressing edges together to seal. Decorate with scraps, brush with beaten egg yolk. Cut two small slits in top to allow steam to escape.
4 Bake in a moderate oven (180°C) for 1½ hours, covering the top with foil if it browns too quickly. Cool and chill in the refrigerator. Serve with salads.

HINT
A food processor makes shortcrust pastry very quickly and gives good results. It is important not to overmix the dough, so turn the machine on in bursts rather than mixing continuously. Place flour and butter in bowl of food processor. Mix for a few seconds until mixture resembles fine breadcrumbs. Add combined water and egg yolk and process until mixture forms a smooth ball, about 30 seconds. Cover and chill for 30 minutes.

Settlers' Chicken

Preparation time:
  10 minutes
Cooking time:
  2 hours
Serves 4

1 x 1.5 kg chicken
5 cups water
1 carrot, sliced
2 stalks celery, sliced
1 onion or leek
2 sprigs parsley
1 onion stuck with
  cloves

1 Place all ingredients in a large saucepan, including giblets if available. Cook with lid on over a low heat until tender, about 2 hours.
2 Lift chicken out and leave stock to cook a little longer to obtain a stronger flavour. Skim fat from top. Reserve stock for soups.
3 Serve hot sliced with parsley sauce or cold with salad.

HINT
Stock may be frozen in ice cube trays for flavouring soups and sauces.

Settlers' Chicken

23

Chicken with Cheese Sauce

Preparation time:
   10 minutes
Cooking time:
   45 minutes
Serves 8

2 kg chicken pieces
pepper
½ cup chicken stock
1 leek, sliced thinly
1 cup cream
175 g blue vein cheese,
   crumbled
½ cup sour cream
¼ cup dry vermouth
½ cup walnut pieces

1 Sprinkle chicken with pepper and place in a baking dish. Bake in a hot oven (200°C) for 25 minutes, turning once. Pour in chicken stock, spoon over chicken and bake another 10 minutes.
2 Place chicken in an ovenproof dish. Keep warm. Place baking dish over medium heat on the stove and remove excess fat. Add leek, cream and cheese and stir until

Chicken with Cheese Sauce

cheese melts. Simmer for a few minutes before stirring in sour cream and vermouth.
3 Pour over the chicken and sprinkle with walnuts. Serve immediately with noodles and a steamed green vegetable.

HINT
Any soft cheese may be used in this sauce. Blue cheese, Brie or Camembert are equally delicious.

Colonial Goose

Preparation time:
  20 minutes
Cooking time:
  2 hours plus 20
  minutes standing
Serves 6

1 x 2.5 kg leg of lamb
90 g butter
1 medium onion, finely
  chopped
2 lamb kidneys
2 cups soft white
  breadcrumbs
2 teaspoons chopped
  fresh rosemary (or
  ½ teaspoon dried)
2 teaspoons chopped
  fresh sage (or
  ½ teaspoon dried)
2 teaspoons chopped
  parsley
finely ground pepper
Gravy
2 tablespoons plain
  flour
1½ cups stock

1 Ask the butcher to
bone the lamb for you.
2 Heat butter and fry
onion until soft and
golden. Skin and core
kidneys and cut into
small dice. Add to pan
and stir until lightly
browned. Remove from
heat and add bread-
crumbs, herbs and
pepper to taste.
3 Allow to cool a little,
then stuff lamb and tie
into a neat shape with
string. Season with
pepper, arrange on a
rack in a baking dish,
and place in a moderate
oven (180°C).
4 Roast uncovered for
about 2 hours for well
done lamb (1½ hours
for medium pink lamb),
basting now and then
with juices that collect in
pan. Allow to rest for 20
minutes before removing
string and carving.
5 To prepare Gravy:
pour off all but 2
tablespoons of dripping
in pan, and stir in flour
over low heat. When
well blended, gradually
stir in stock and
continue stirring until
gravy is smooth and
thickened. Taste for
seasoning and strain into
a gravy boat.

HINT
For a rich brown
gravy add flour to
pan, blend until
smooth, reduce heat
to low and stir
constantly until flour
mixture turns a rich
brown colour, taking
care not to burn.

Savoury Beef Olives

Preparation time:
  30 minutes
Cooking time:
  1¼ hours
Serves 4

4 slices (500 g) very thin
  sliced topside
1 cup soft breadcrumbs
2 tablespoons chopped
  parsley
1 small apple, peeled
  and chopped finely
1 bacon rasher, chopped
  finely
½ teaspoon dried
  caraway seeds
pepper
2 tablespoons seasoned
  flour
2 tablespoons oil
2 large carrots, sliced
1 large onion, sliced
1½ cups beef stock
2 tablespoons tomato
  paste
1 bay leaf

1 Trim steak if
necessary and cut into
10 cm squares. Combine
breadcrumbs, parsley,
apple, bacon, seeds and
pepper to taste. Divide
between the meat slices,
roll up and secure with
strong cotton. Roll in
seasoned flour.
2 Heat oil and brown
meat rolls all over. Place
in a greased ovenproof
dish together with
carrots and onion and
sprinkle over any
remaining flour.
3 Mix together beef
stock and tomato paste.
Add bay leaf and pour
into dish. Cover and
bake in a moderately
slow oven (160°C) for
1–1¼ hours until
tender. Remove cotton
before serving.

Shearers' Stew with Dumplings

Preparation time:
  20 minutes
Cooking time:
  2 hours
Serves 6

1 tablespoon oil
30 g butter
1 kg leg of lamb, boned,
  cubed and rolled in
  seasoned flour
3 onions, quartered
3 parsnips, sliced thickly
3 carrots, sliced thickly
2 sticks celery, chopped
meat or vegetable stock
  or water
3 tablespoons chopped
  parsley
¾ teaspoon mixed herbs
1 tablespoon
  Worcestershire sauce
pepper and a pinch of
  sugar

1 Heat oil and butter in
a large heavy frying pan
and brown meat, adding
a little extra oil if
necessary. Push to one
side and sauté onions
until transparent.
2 Transfer to a heavy
saucepan, adding bits
left in bottom of frying
pan blended with a little
stock or water. Add
parsnips, carrots and
celery and sufficient
stock or water to barely
cover, along with

Shearers' Stew with Dumplings

26

parsley, herbs,
Worcestershire sauce,
pepper and sugar.
Simmer on low heat for
about 2 hours or until
meat is tender.
3 Serve with Jumbuck
Dumplings.

Jumbuck Dumplings

Preparation time:
   10 minutes
Cooking time:
   15 minutes
Serves 6

2 cups self-raising flour
1 tablespoon chopped
   parsley
plenty of black pepper
about ¾ cup milk or
   water

1 Put flour, parsley and
pepper in a bowl and stir
in milk or water until
dough forms a soft
dropping consistency.
With floury palms
lightly roll mixture into
balls and place on top of
stew while it is
simmering.
2 Cover and cook for
about 15 minutes before
ready to serve stew.

27

Pork Madeira

Preparation time:
  20 minutes
Cooking time:
  15 minutes
Serves 6

1 kg pork fillets
2 tablespoons flour
freshly ground pepper
2 tablespoons vegetable
  oil
1 tablespoon butter
1 onion, chopped
375 g button
  mushrooms
30 g butter, extra
½ cup unsweetened
  apple juice
½ cup cream
½ cup Madeira
1 tablespoon tomato
  paste

1 Cut pork into thick pieces and toss in the flour, seasoned with pepper.
2 Heat oil and 1 tablespoon of butter together, add onion and cook slowly until just changing colour. Stir in mushrooms and cook a few more minutes. Remove onion and mushrooms from pan.
3 Heat extra butter, add pork and cook quickly for 7–10 minutes. Stir in onion and mushrooms and cook for 1 minute. Add apple juice, cream, Madeira and tomato paste and stir until thickened.

4 Serve with rice or potatoes and salad.

HINT
For a richer sauce replace apple juice with apple purée or bottled apple sauce.

Rich Casserole of Beef

Preparation time:
  20 minutes
Cooking time:
  2 hours
Serves 4

750 g chuck steak,
  cubed
2 tablespoons plain flour
pepper
2 tablespoons oil
1 cup red wine
1 bay leaf
1 teaspoon fresh thyme
1 clove garlic, crushed
2 tablespoons tomato
  paste
1 teaspoon juniper
  berries, optional
12 small onions
2 carrots, sliced
1 stalk celery, sliced
1 leek, sliced

1 Toss meat in flour seasoned with pepper and coat evenly. Brown in hot oil all over and then transfer to an ovenproof dish.
2 Stir wine into pan, scraping well to mix in any flour or brown pieces left in the bottom. Add bay leaf, thyme, garlic, tomato paste and juniper berries. Mix well and pour over meat. Cover with lid and cook gently in a moderate oven (180°C) for 1 hour.
3 Add onions, carrots and celery and cook for another 30 minutes. Add leeks and cook until meat is tender, about 20–30 minutes.

HINT
Dried juniper berries, small purple-black berries with a distinctive flavour, are available from health food stores and speciality cookware shops. Crush before adding to a dish for maximum flavour.

Rich Casserole of Beef

Plum-glazed Corned Beef

Preparation time:
    10 minutes
Cooking time:
    1 hour and 40 minutes
Serves 6

1.5 kg corned silverside
1 tablespoon brown
    sugar
1 tablespoon vinegar
1 clove garlic, sliced
1 onion studded with 4
    cloves
4 peppercorns
1 bouquet garni (1 bay
    leaf, sprigs of thyme
    and parsley)
4 carrots
4 small onions, peeled
4 potatoes
4 medium parsnips
1 cup bottled plum sauce
1 teaspoon honey
1 tablespoon orange
    juice

1   Put corned beef in a
heavy saucepan with
brown sugar, vinegar,
garlic, onion with
cloves, peppercorns and
bouquet garni. Add
enough water to cover.
Heat until boiling, cover
and simmer 40 minutes.
Add carrots, onions,
potatoes and parsnips.
Simmer for approxi-
mately 1 hour more or
until meat is tender.
Remove vegetables when
cooked, drain and keep
warm. Reserve parsnips.

2 Meanwhile melt plum sauce, honey and orange juice over hot water, blend and keep warm.

3 Transfer meat to a heated platter and brush with plum glaze. Serve meat sliced and surrounded by vegetables, with Parsnip Cakes made from reserved parsnips. A green vegetable and mustard or horseradish sauce go well with this dish. (See page 46 for Parsnip Cake recipe.)

HINT

A purée of stewed fresh plums or peaches may replace bottled plum sauce. A little extra orange juice may be needed to obtain a sauce consistency.

Plum-Glazed Corned Beef and Parsnip Cakes

Rabbit Casserole

Preparation time:
    40 minutes plus
    8 hours soaking
Cooking time:
    1½ hours
Serves 4

1 rabbit, cut into
    serving pieces
2 teaspoons vinegar
plain flour, seasoned
    with salt and pepper
1 tablespoon oil
1 tablespoon butter
3 medium onions,
    coarsely chopped
3 rashers streaky bacon,
    diced
1 tablespoon plain flour
1 cup dry white wine
½ cup chicken stock
1 tablespoon tomato
    paste
3 sprigs parsley
2 sprigs thyme
1 bay leaf
freshly ground pepper
125 g button
    mushrooms, halved
    or sliced
1 tablespoon extra
    butter
chopped parsley

1 Soak rabbit for 6–8 hours in cold salted water with the vinegar added. Drain and dry thoroughly, then coat with seasoned flour.
2 Heat together the oil and butter, add the rabbit pieces and brown all over. Transfer rabbit to ovenproof dish. Add onions and bacon to the pan and gently fry until onions have softened. Add the flour, stir for a minute or two, then pour in the wine and chicken stock. Add the tomato paste and stir until boiling. Pour over rabbit in dish, and add the parsley, thyme and bay leaf, tied together, with pepper to taste.
3 Cover and cook in a moderately slow oven (160°C) for about 1½ hours, or until tender. Just before cooking time is finished, quickly fry the mushrooms in extra butter for a minute or two and mix into the casserole. Remove the bundle of herbs and serve casserole garnished with chopped parsley.

Rabbit Terrine

Preparation time:
    3 hours
Cooking time:
    1¼ hours
Serves 8

meat from back legs and
    saddles of 2 rabbits,
    minced and marinated
    a few hours in ¼ cup
    brandy
2 rabbit or chicken
    livers, finely chopped
500 g streaky pork belly,
    minced
1 white onion, finely
    chopped and sautéed
    in 1 tablespoon butter
125 g chopped
    mushrooms
1 teaspoon chopped
    fresh rosemary
1 teaspoon chopped
    fresh parsley
½ cup white wine
pepper
½ teaspoon ground
    nutmeg
2 tablespoons cream
2 bay leaves
6 rashers bacon, rinds
    removed

1 In a bowl combine all ingredients except bay leaves and bacon. Line an ovenproof terrine with the bacon, leaving ends of rashers overlapping sides. Fill terrine with mixture.
2 Place bay leaves on top and bring overlapping bacon ends over top. Bake in a baking dish half full of water in a moderate oven (180°C) 1 to 1¼ hours or until juices run clear when tested with a skewer. Cool and serve with salad.

HINT
Serve Rabbit Terrine with these tasty herb toasts. Rub French bread slices with garlic, brush with olive oil and sprinkle with fresh or dried mixed herbs of your choice. Arrange on a baking tray and cook in moderate oven till golden and crisp.

Rabbit Terrine

Lamb Pilaf

Lamb Pilaf

Preparation time:
  15 minutes
Cooking time:
  30 minutes
Serves 4

500 g lamb fillets, cubed
90 g ghee or butter
1 onion, chopped
1 carrot, cut into
  julienne strips
pepper
2 cups rice
3½ cups boiling chicken
  stock

½ cup raisins
sliced raw onion
chopped parsley

1 Brown meat in ghee or butter. Stir in onion and carrot and cook for a few minutes. Season to taste with pepper, add rice and stir until coated with ghee.
2 Pour over boiling stock. Reduce heat. Cover with a tight-fitting lid and cook until rice is tender and liquid has been absorbed, about 20 minutes. Add raisins, replace lid and leave until plumped.
3 Garnish with onion slices and chopped parsley and serve.

HINT
Ghee or clarified butter is butter with milk solids and salts removed. It can be heated to a high temperature without burning.

Aussie Meat Pies

Preparation time:
  40 minutes
Cooking time:
  20 minutes
Makes 4 x 10 cm pies

250 g puff pastry
1 tablespoon butter
1 onion, finely chopped
250 g minced beef
1 tablespoon plain flour
2 tablespoons
  Worcestershire sauce
2 tablespoons water
salt and pepper
beaten egg for glazing

1 Roll pastry out thinly, cut into rounds and line four 10 cm pie tins.
2 Heat the butter and gently fry the onion until transparent. Add beef and stir until browned. Stir in flour, sauce, water, salt and pepper, and bring to boil. Remove from the heat and cool.
3 Divide fillings between the 4 tins, cut 4 rounds from remaining pastry and cover each pie, crimping edges. Make a vent with a skewer in the centre of each and decorate with pastry trimmings. Brush with beaten egg. Stand tins on a baking tray; bake in a moderately hot oven 210°C (190°C gas) for 20 minutes until cooked.
4 Serve with tomato sauce or, for a more substantial meal, with creamy mashed potatoes and peas.

Aussie Meat Pie

Turkey Tetrazzini

Preparation time:
   40 minutes
Cooking time:
   15 minutes
Serves 4

250 g pink, green or
   white tagliatelle or a
   mixture of all three
60 g butter
125 g mushrooms,
   thinly sliced
1 small onion, grated
¼ cup plain flour
1 cup evaporated milk
1½ cups chicken stock
2 tablespoons dry sherry
pepper
1 small green and 1
   small red capsicum,
   cut into short thin
   strips
2 cups diced cooked
   turkey
½ cup grated Parmesan
   cheese

1 Cook the tagliatelle in plenty of boiling salted water until tender. Drain and arrange in a greased ovenproof dish.
2 Melt half the butter, add the mushrooms and fry gently until softened. Add the rest of the butter and the onion and cook for 20 seconds. Stir in the flour and cook for 1 minute. Slowly stir in the evaporated milk and the stock and cook, stirring, until boiling. Add the sherry, season with pepper, and simmer for 1–2 minutes.
3 Drop the strips of capsicum into a small pan of cold water and slowly bring to the boil. Drain and add to the sauce. Pour half the sauce over the pasta, mixing in. Add the turkey to the rest of the sauce and pour into the dish. Sprinkle with the grated cheese and bake in a moderate oven (180°C) for about 15 minutes. Serve with a green salad.

HINT
Try using cold cooked chicken, flaked tuna or cooked smoked cod in this recipe.

Turkey Tetrazzini

=VEGETABLES, SALADS AND BREADS=

Bush Damper

*W*hether they are to accompany a main dish or to be eaten as a separate course, vegetables and salads provide additional colour, flavour and texture to a meal. They are also a source of essential minerals, vitamins and fibre in our daily diet.

We seem to be most fortunate in having a bountiful selection of vegetables available the year round. These recipes will help you to make imaginative use of not only staples like potato, parsnip and pumpkin but also zucchini, eggplant and capsicum.

Also included in this section are some traditional recipes for damper and scones, delicious to eat when warm with lashings of butter.

Bush Damper

Preparation time:
  15 minutes
Cooking time:
  30 minutes
Makes 1 large damper

3 cups self-raising flour
2 teaspoons salt
45 g butter
½ cup milk
½ cup water

1 Sift flour and salt into a bowl and rub in butter until mixture resembles fine crumbs. Make a well in centre, add combined milk and water and mix lightly with a knife until dough leaves sides of bowl.
2 Gently knead on a lightly floured surface and then knead into a round. Put on a greased oven tray and pat into a round 15–16 cm in diameter.
3 Bake in a moderately hot oven 210°C (190°C gas) for 10 minutes. Reduce heat to 180°C and bake another 20 minutes.

HINT
Eat the day it is made. Bush Damper is traditionally served with "cocky's joy" (golden syrup) and billy tea. For variation, add ¾ cup grated Cheddar cheese.

Irish Soda Bread

Preparation time:
  20 minutes
Cooking time:
  35 minutes
Serves 6

15 g butter
1 cup self-raising flour
2 cups plain flour
1 teaspoon salt
1 teaspoon bicarbonate
  of soda
1 cup cooked sieved
  potato
1 egg
1¼ cups buttermilk

1 Rub butter into sifted dry ingredients. Mix in potato.
2 Mix in egg beaten with half the buttermilk and gradually stir in enough remaining buttermilk to form a soft dough.
3 Place dough in a greased 20 cm sandwich cake tin, cut a cross in the top with a sharp knife and bake in a moderate oven (180°C) for 35 minutes or until cooked. For a soft crust, brush while hot with melted butter.

HINT
Do not mash potato with butter or milk. Serve with lashings of butter.

39

Stuffed Vegetables

Preparation time:
20 minutes
Cooking time:
20 minutes
Serves 6

3 large well-shaped
capsicums
30 g butter

1 medium onion, finely
chopped
1 clove garlic, crushed
1/4 teaspoon dried basil
1 tablespoon tomato
paste
1/4 cup cream
1 egg, beaten
2 tablespoons
wheatgerm
freshly ground pepper
1 x 250 g can 3-bean
mix drained

1/2 cup small shell
macaroni, cooked and
drained
1/2 cup grated Parmesan
cheese

1 Cut tops off
capsicums. Scoop out
seeds and membrane.
Plunge in boiling water
1 minute. Refresh
under cold running
water and drain.
2 Melt butter in small

Pumpkin Scone Wedge and Stuffed Vegetables

pan and fry onion, garlic and basil until onion is transparent. Add tomato paste, cream, egg, wheatgerm and pepper. Mix well. Stir in beans and macaroni.
3 Stand capsicums upright in baking dish. Spoon bean filling evenly into each capsicum. Sprinkle with cheese and bake in moderate 180°C oven for 15–20 minutes.

Hint
Zucchini, eggplant and tomatoes may be filled and baked in the same way, but eggplant and tomatoes do not need blanching.

Pumpkin Scone Wedge

Preparation time:
   30 minutes
Cooking time:
   25 minutes
Serves 6

30 g butter
2 tablespoons sugar
1 cup mashed, well-
   drained, cooked
   pumpkin
1 egg
2 cups self-raising flour
pinch salt
1/3 cup sultanas
milk for glazing

1 Beat together butter and sugar until creamy. Mix in pumpkin and egg.
2 Sift flour and salt and mix in together with sultanas.
3 Knead lightly on a floured surface. Pat into a 20cm round and place on a lightly greased oven tray. Cut into 8 sections almost to the bottom so that they can be pulled apart when baked. Brush with milk and bake in a moderately hot oven (210°C) for 20–25 minutes.

Hint
For this recipe butternut pumpkin would be ideal, giving a very sweet taste and good colour.

Luncheon Bouquet

Preparation time:
  30 minutes
Cooking time: nil
Serves 4

125 g mushrooms
1 tablespoon lemon juice
endive or lettuce of your
  choice
8 canned asparagus
  spears
1 ripe avocado, sliced
1 cup sliced celery
2 hard-boiled eggs,
  quartered
½ cup thinly sliced
  cucumber
1 small Spanish onion,
  sliced thinly
½ cup pecans
2 cups cooked brown
  rice, chilled
1 punnet cherry
  tomatoes
Horseradish Dressing
¼ cup whole egg
  mayonnaise
3 tablespoons cream
1 teaspoon horseradish
  cream

1 Slice mushrooms and
sprinkle with lemon
juice. Arrange endive on
four salad plates with
asparagus spears and
sliced avocado.
2 Combine celery, hard-
boiled eggs, cucumber,
onion, pecans, rice,
tomatoes and
mushrooms. Pile onto
salad plates and chill
thoroughly.
3 Combine dressing

ingredients and pour
over salad just before
serving. Serve with
crusty bread.

Sweet Potato Purée

Preparation time:
  5 minutes
Cooking time:
  20 minutes
Serves 6

5 large red or white
  sweet potatoes,
  coarsely chopped
3 Granny Smith apples,
  peeled, cored and
  chopped
½ cup evaporated milk,
  heated
30g melted butter
pinch of nutmeg
pepper

1 Cook potatoes in
boiling water until
tender; drain
thoroughly.
2 Cook apples gently in
½ cup water until
tender; drain well
3 Mash potatoes and
purée apples. Combine
with hot evaporated
milk, melted butter and
nutmeg, seasoning with
pepper to taste.
4 Whisk until smooth
and pile into a warmed
serving bowl. This is
good with roast veal,
lamb, pork or chicken,
and with pork chops.

Bubble and Squeak

Preparation time:
  20 minutes
Cooking time:
  20 minutes
Serves 2

30 g butter
1 cup shredded corned
  beef
½ cup cubed cooked
  potato
½ cup cubed cooked
  carrot
½ cup cubed cooked
  parsnip
½ cup shredded cooked
  cabbage
2 eggs
parsley

1 Heat butter in a
heavy-based pan, add
corned beef, potato,
carrot, parsnip and
cabbage and cook,
stirring, 1 minute.
2 Press beef and
vegetable mixture evenly
over pan, cook over a
medium heat until
browned on both sides
and formed into a cake.
3 Poach or fry eggs and
serve on top of Bubble
and Squeak. Garnish
with parsley.

HINT
Any cold cooked
vegetables or meats
may be used in
Bubble and Squeak.

Bubble and Squeak

Ratatouille

Ratatouille

Preparation time:
  1 hour
Cooking time:
  30–40 minutes
Serves 6

1 eggplant
salt
3 tablespoons olive oil
500 g zucchini, sliced
2 onions, sliced
1 red capsicum, sliced
500 g tomatoes,
  chopped

1 clove garlic, crushed
2 tablespoons chopped
  parsley
freshly ground black
  pepper

1 Cut eggplant into slices. Place in a colander. Sprinkle with salt and leave 1 hour. Rinse and pat dry.
2 Heat oil in a heavy frypan. Add eggplant, sliced zucchini, onions and capsicum and cook for a few minutes. Add tomatoes, garlic, parsley and pepper to taste.

3 Cover with a tight-fitting lid and cook a little longer until vegetables are tender but crisp. Do not overcook.
4 Serve ratatouille with pasta shells, green salad and crusty bread.

HINT
Eggplant is salted and left to stand to extract bitter juices. Rinse well and dry eggplant slices with absorbent paper before cooking.

Savoury Horseshoe

Preparation time:
40 minutes
Cooking time:
20 minutes
Serves 12

2 cups self-raising flour
pinch salt
30 g butter or
  margarine, cut into
  small pieces
½ cup milk
½ cup water

Filling
1 cup shredded tasty
  cheese
1 tomato, peeled and
  diced
2 gherkins, chopped
½ small onion, chopped
¼ cup chopped
  capsicum
6 to 8 stuffed olives,
  chopped
seasonings to taste
½ cup shredded tasty
  cheese, extra

1 Preheat oven to 210°C (190°C gas). Sift flour and salt into large bowl. Add butter and rub lightly into flour using fingertips.

2 Combine milk and water. Make a well in the centre of the flour and pour in all liquid (reserve a teaspoon for glazing). Mix quickly into a soft dough.

3 Turn onto a floured board (use self-raising flour to dust). Knead lightly. Roll out gently to form a rectangle about 1.5 cm thick.

4 To prepare filling: combine the cheese, tomato, gherkins, onion, capsicum, olives and seasonings.

5 Spread filling over dough. Roll up as a Swiss roll. Place seam side down on a greased oven tray.

6 Form into a horseshoe shape. Slit dough at 2 cm intervals with a sharp knife and sprinkle with extra cheese. Bake for 15–20 minutes.

Savoury Horseshoe

2 teaspoons chopped
   fresh basil
¼ cup sultanas
½ cup chopped walnuts
1 cup natural yoghurt
1 clove garlic, crushed

Slice or chop cucumber
into pieces and combine
with all other
ingredients. Place in
salad bowl and serve.

Walnut Avocado Salad

Preparation time:
   15 minutes
Cooking time: nil
Serves 4

assorted lettuce leaves
3 small ripe avocados
½ cup walnut pieces
2 teaspoons white wine
   vinegar
1 teaspoon French
   mustard
freshly gound pepper
2 tablespoons walnut oil
½ cup raisins

1 Arrange lettuce leaves
on individual serving
plates. Peel avocados
and cut into slices.
Sprinkle over walnuts.
2 Beat together vinegar,
mustard and pepper.
Add oil a drop at a
time, beating
continuously so that
the dressing is thick.
Add raisins, pour over
avocado and serve.

Parsnip Cakes

Parsnip Cakes

Preparation time:
   30 minutes
Cooking time:
   10 minutes
Makes 6 cakes

4 medium parsnips,
   cooked and mashed
4 tablespoons self-
   raising flour
1 egg, beaten
pepper and dash of
   nutmeg
butter for frying

1 Mix mashed parsnips
with flour, egg, pepper
and nutmeg.
2 Form into cakes with
floury hands and fry on
both sides in butter until
brown and crisp. Drain
on kitchen paper.
3 Serve with Plum-
Glazed Corned Beef.

Note. Do not mash
parsnips with butter or
milk for this recipe as a
dry parsnip base is
needed.

Crunchy Cucumber Salad

Preparation time:
   15 minutes
Cooking time: nil
Serves 4

1 large green cucumber
1 cup chopped shallots
1 tablespoon chopped
   fresh mint

Corn and Bacon Hotpot

Preparation time:
   20 minutes
Cooking time:
   25 minutes
Serves 4

250 g bacon, cut into
   wide strips
2 onions, sliced

1 clove garlic, crushed
1 x 400 g can tomatoes
4 small potatoes, sliced
pepper
4 fresh or frozen corn
   cobs

1 Cook bacon in its own fat until browned. Remove from pan. Add onion and garlic to pan and cook for a few minutes. Stir in undrained tomatoes, sliced potatoes, pepper to taste and the bacon. Cook gently with the lid on 10–15 minutes.
2 Slice the corn cobs and press into the hotpot, adding a small amount of vegetable stock if necessary. Cover pot and cook until corn is tender, about 10 minutes.

Corn and Bacon Hotpot

DESSERTS

Orange Snow with Lemon Sauce

*F*ew things inspire more nostalgia than the puddings of childhood, like Queen of Puddings or Bread and Butter Custard. Here we have a few traditional and old-time country puddings together with some delectable cold sweets. Whether you choose a hot or cold dessert any of these recipes makes a perfect end to a meal.

Orange Snow with Lemon Sauce

Preparation time:
  35 minutes
Cooking time: nil
Serves 8

3 eggs, separated
½ cup caster sugar
1 cup milk, heated
3 teaspoons gelatine, softened in a little water
1 cup orange juice
300 mL cream
Lemon Sauce
1 egg yolk
¼ cup sugar
60 g butter, softened
2 teaspoons cornflour
½ cup orange juice
¼ cup lemon juice

1 Beat egg yolks and sugar together. Add hot milk and stir thoroughly. Pour into a saucepan and stir over a low heat until hot and almost boiling.
2 Add softened gelatine and stir until dissolved.
3 Pour into a bowl and stir over chilled water until cold. Stir in orange juice. Beat egg whites until stiff and whip cream until thick. Fold both into orange mixture until evenly mixed.
4 Pour into a glass serving dish and chill thoroughly. Serve with peeled orange slices flavoured with orange brandy liqueur and chilled thoroughly, and Lemon Sauce.
5 To make Lemon Sauce: place all ingredients in a saucepan and whisk together thoroughly. Stir over a low heat until thickened and boiling. Remove from heat, and stir over chilled water until cold. If sauce is too thick, thin with a little cream.

HINT
To soften gelatine, sprinkle it over hot water to dissolve, then cool to room temperature.

Bread and Butter Custard

Preparation time:
  30 minutes
Cooking time:
  40 minutes
Serves 4

4–5 slices white bread
butter
½ cup sultanas
3 eggs
2 cups milk
2 tablespoons sugar
1 teaspoon vanilla essence
nutmeg

1 Spread the bread with butter and either leave whole or cut into fingers.
2 Place sultanas in a greased ovenproof dish and cover with bread. Beat eggs, milk, sugar and vanilla together and pour over bread. Allow to stand 20 minutes.
3 Sprinkle with nutmeg and bake in a moderate oven 35–40 minutes. Serve warm with apple sauce.

HINT
Spread bread with strawberry or raspberry jam for a delicious variation of this recipe.

Queen of Puddings

Preparation time:
  15 minutes
Cooking time:
  55 minutes
Serves 6

1 cup soft white
  breadcrumbs
2 cups milk, scalded
2 eggs, separated
⅓ cup sugar
3 tablespoons
  strawberry jam
1 cup sliced strawberries

1 Place breadcrumbs in a bowl with hot milk and let stand for 10 minutes. Beat egg yolks with half the sugar and stir into crumb mixture.
2 Spoon custard into a greased ovenproof dish and bake in a moderately slow oven for 45 minutes, or until firm to the touch.
3 Combine strawberry jam and sliced straw-berries and spread over custard. Whip egg whites until stiff and then beat in remaining sugar to form a meringue.
4 Swirl meringue over top. Increase oven temperature to moderately hot, and bake pudding for 8–10 minutes, or until meringue is set and lightly browned. Serve hot or warm, by itself or with pouring cream.

Liqueur Soufflé

Preparation time:
  30 minutes
Cooking time:
  40 minutes
Serves 6

¼ cup caster sugar
1½ tablespoons plain
  flour
¾ cup milk
¼ cup Orange Curaçao
15 g butter
5 egg yolks, beaten
7 egg whites

1 Stir sugar and flour together in a saucepan. Gradually add milk and stir over a low heat until boiling and thickened.
2 Remove from heat, stir in liqueur and butter. Pour a little of the hot mixture onto the beaten yolks, stirring well. Return all to saucepan and beat until evenly mixed.
3 Beat egg whites until thick and gently fold into yolk mixture. Pour into a greased and lightly sprinkled with sugar 6-cup soufflé dish.
4 Bake in a moderately hot oven 35–40 minutes until outside is firm and inside creamy. Serve immediately with top sprinkled with sifted icing sugar.

Liqueur Soufflé

Crème Caramel

Preparation time:
  20 minutes plus
  overnight setting time
Cooking time: 25 minutes
Serves 6

1 cup caster sugar
½ cup water
1½ cups milk
½ cup cream
⅓ cup sugar
4 eggs, beaten
1 teaspoon vanilla
  essence

1 Place caster sugar and water in a small saucepan and stir over a low heat until sugar dissolves. Cook without stirring until golden brown and remove from heat immediately. Take care not to burn. Pour quickly into 6 individual greased moulds and rotate to coat the sides.
2 Heat milk and cream together. Add the ⅓ cup sugar and stir until dissolved. Cool to lukewarm. Pour onto beaten eggs and vanilla and mix well.
3 Pour into caramel-lined moulds and place in a baking tin half filled with warm water. Bake in a moderate oven 20–25 minutes until set. Remove from water and allow to cool.
4 Chill in refrigerator overnight. Run a knife carefully around sides if unmoulding, or serve straight from dishes.

Crème Caramel

Mango Jelly

Preparation time:
  30 minutes plus
  overnight setting time
Cooking time: nil
Serves 4

1 large ripe mango
2 tablespoons sherry
¼ cup orange juice
1 tablespoon lemon juice
¼ cup icing sugar, sifted
3 teaspoons gelatine
¾ cup thickened cream,
  whipped
pawpaw, melon wedges,
  kiwi fruit and
  passionfruit, for
  decoration

1 Peel mango, cut flesh from stone and pulverise in a processor. Tip into a basin and stir in sherry, orange and lemon juice, and icing sugar.
2 Soften gelatine in a little cold water and stir over hot water until dissolved. Cool.
3 Fold into mango mixture together with whipped cream.
4 Pour into a wet or lightly oiled 4-cup mould and chill until set. Unmould onto a serving platter and surround with pawpaw and melon wedges, sliced kiwi fruit and passionfruit.

Mango Jelly

CAKES AND PIES

Soldiers' Christmas Cake

*C*akes and pies 'like Grandma used to make' are favourites with everyone. Our society now consists of people from many other countries. They have brought with them their favourite family recipes to be shared. These recipes have been absorbed into our gastronomic culture, and some of the best are included here. These mouth-watering delicacies will be asked for again and again.

Soldiers' Christmas Cake

Preparation time:
1 hour
Cooking time:
3 hours
Makes 1 x 20 cm cake

250 g seeded raisins, chopped
250 g sultanas
250 g currants
125 g glacé cherries, chopped
125 g chopped mixed peel
125 g blanched almonds, chopped
⅔ cup brandy or orange juice
2 cups plain flour
½ cup self-raising flour
½ teaspoon nutmeg
½ teaspoon cinnamon
1 teaspoon mixed spice
250 g butter
1½ cups brown sugar
2 tablespoons jam or marmalade
4 eggs

1 Combine seeded raisins with sultanas, currants, cherries, mixed peel and almonds. Sprinkle with brandy or orange juice.
2 Sift flours with spices. Beat butter and brown sugar until light and fluffy. Add jam and beat again. Add eggs, one at a time, beating well after each addition.
3 Fold in fruit and flour mixtures alternately. Mix thoroughly. Spoon into a deep 20 cm round cake tin, lined with two layers each of foil and greaseproof paper, or use brown paper. Bake in a moderate oven (180°C) for 30 minutes. Reduce heat to moderately slow (160°C) and cook for 2½–3 hours. Test with fine skewer before removing from oven.

HINT
Fruit may be measured and soaked in brandy several weeks in advance.

Cinnamon Tea Cake

Preparation time:
20 minutes
Cooking time:
30 minutes
Makes 1 cake

1 cup self-raising flour
½ teaspoon cinnamon
¼ teaspoon nutmeg
1 egg, separated
½ cup sugar
½ cup milk
vanilla essence
30 g butter, melted
extra melted butter
1 teaspoon cinnamon, extra
1 tablespoon sugar, extra

1 Sift flour with the ½ teaspoon of cinnamon and the nutmeg.
2 Beat egg white until stiff. Add egg yolk and mix in. Gradually beat in the ½ cup of sugar. Slowly stir in milk and vanilla essence.
3 Stir in sifted dry ingredients, with melted butter. Spoon into a greased 18 cm round sandwich tin and bake in a moderate oven (180°C) for 30 minutes. While still hot, brush the top with extra melted butter and sprinkle with extra cinnamon and sugar. Serve warm or cold, with butter.

Coffee Butter Cake

Preparation time:
    10 minutes
Cooking time:
    40 minutes
Makes 1 cake

1¼ *cups self-raising
    flour*
¾ *cup lightly filled
    brown sugar*
2 *teaspoons instant
    coffee powder*
90 g *butter, melted*
2 *eggs*

3 *tablespoons cream*
100 g *chocolate
blanched almonds*

1 Place flour, sugar and instant coffee in a bowl. Stir in melted butter, eggs and cream and beat until smooth.
2 Pour into a greased 19cm x 21cm loaf tin and bake in a moderate oven (180°C) for 35–40 minutes until cooked. Cool on a wire rack.
3 Melt chocolate gently, spread over top of cake and decorate with almonds.

Coffee Butter Cake

Apple Cheesecake

Preparation time:
    10 minutes
Cooking time:
    25 minutes
Serves 8

¾ *cup plain flour*
60 g *butter, softened*
2 *teaspoons water*
red jam
2 *apples, peeled, cored
    and sliced*
¼ *cup sultanas*
1 *cup cottage cheese,
    sieved*
½ *cup plain flour*
½ *cup sugar*
3 *eggs*
grated rind of 1 lemon
1 *tablespoon lemon juice*
½ *cup cream, whipped*
icing sugar

1 Mix flour, butter and water together into a dough. Press evenly onto base of a greased 23 cm springform tin. Spread with jam. Cover with apple slices and half the sultanas.
2 Beat together cottage cheese, flour, sugar, eggs, lemon rind, juice and remaining sultanas. Fold in whipped cream and pour over the apples.
3 Bake in a hot oven 210°C (190°C gas) for 25 minutes, until set and lightly brown. Sift icing sugar over top and serve cheesecake warm.

Apple Cheesecake

Little Lemon Tarts

Preparation time:
   15 minutes plus 30
   minutes standing time
Cooking time:
   15 minutes
Makes 20 tarts

1 ¼ *cups plain flour*
2 *tablespoons caster*
   sugar
125 *g butter*
1 *egg yolk*
1 *tablespoon lemon juice*

Lemon Butter
125 *g butter*
1 *cup sugar*
finely grated rind of 3
   medium lemons
½ *cup lemon juice*
4 *eggs, lightly beaten*

1 Sift flour and sugar together. Add butter and rub in until mixture resembles fine breadcrumbs.
2 Combine egg yolk with lemon juice and add to flour mixture. Mix together and knead gently to form a smooth ball. Wrap and chill for 30 minutes.
3 Roll out on a floured surface and cut in circles to line fluted tartlet tins. Bake in a moderate oven (180°C) for 12–15 minutes or until light golden. Remove from tins and leave to cool before serving. Fill with Lemon Butter and serve with whipped cream.
4 To prepare Lemon Butter: melt butter over hot water. Add sugar and stir until dissolved. Mix in lemon rind and juice. Quickly stir in eggs. Stir over boiling water until mixture is thick enough to coat the back of a wooden spoon, about 5 minutes. Strain, pour into hot sterilised jars and seal. When cold, store in refrigerator until needed.

HINT
A layer of prepared marzipan topped with jam makes a rich and delicious tart filling.

Little Lemon Tarts

Edinburgh Shortbread

Edinburgh Shortbread

Preparation time:
  15 minutes
Cooking time:
  20 minutes
Makes 2 x 20 cm rounds

250 g butter
½ cup caster sugar

2¼ cups plain flour
½ cup rice flour

1 Cream butter and sugar. Gradually add flours and work with hands into a smooth creamy ball.
2 Press out on oven trays lined with baking paper to form 2 x 20 cm rounds, 1cm thick. Pinch a frill around the edge and mark lightly into 8 wedges. Pierce all over with a fork.
3 Bake in a moderately slow oven (160°C) for 20 minutes until a pale straw colour. Cool slightly and then cut through or break at the marked lines.

French Apple Tart

French Apple Tart

Preparation time:
  20 minutes
Cooking time:
  30 minutes
Makes 1 x 28 cm tart

*1 x 375g packet frozen
  puff pastry, thawed
4 cooking apples, peeled
  and sliced thinly
½ cup apricot jam
1 tablespoon white wine
  or water*

1. Roll out pastry into a circle and line a shallow 28 cm pie plate or pizza tray. Cover with apple slices, overlapping and placed close together.
2. Heat jam and wine together and carefully brush over apple slices. Bake in hot oven (200°C) for 25–30 minutes, brushing now and again with remaining jam. At the end of cooking time, place under a hot grill to give a glazed look if desired. Serve warm.

Apple Marmalade Pie

Preparation time:
  30 minutes
Cooking time:
  50 minutes
Makes 1 x 23 cm pie

*1½ cups flour
150 g butter
2 tablespoons hot water*

*1 kg Granny Smith
  apples, peeled and
  sliced
3 tablespoons
  marmalade
2–3 cloves
½ cup caster sugar
unbeaten egg white
extra sugar
ground cinnamon*

1 Sift flour, add the butter melted in the hot water and blend, adding flour or more hot water until mixture is a workable consistency. Roll out lightly on a floured board and line a 23 cm springform cake tin.
2 Mix together sliced apples, marmalade, cloves and sugar and spread over pastry case.
3 Brush edges with hot water and cover with remaining pastry, pressing edges together to seal. Decorate with pastry trimmings and make a vent in the centre for steam to escape.
4 Brush with unbeaten egg white, sprinkle generously with sugar and bake in a moderately hot oven (190°C) for 40–50 minutes until pastry is golden brown. Cover with foil if pastry is browning too much. When ready to serve, dust with cinnamon. Serve hot or cold with whipped sweetened cream flavoured with cinnamon.

Apple Marmalade Pie

Honey Cake

Preparation time:
  20 minutes
Cooking time:
  50 minutes
Makes 1 x 20 cm cake

2 cups plain flour
½ teaspoon bicarbonate of soda
1 teaspoon cinnamon
1 teaspoon ground cardamom
1 teaspoon ground ginger
½ teaspoon ground cloves
3 eggs
½ cup vegetable oil
¾ cup honey
¾ cup lightly filled dark brown sugar
preserved ginger, sliced
Lemon Icing
1 cup icing sugar
1 teaspoon Copha
lemon juice

1 Sift dry ingredients into large bowl of electric mixer. Add all remaining ingredients and beat 5 minutes.

2 Pour into a greased 20 cm ring cake tin. Bake in a moderate oven (180°C) until cooked, about 50 minutes. Cool and ice with thin Lemon Icing and decorate with sliced preserved ginger.

3 To make Lemon Icing: put sifted icing sugar in a small saucepan with Copha and enough lemon juice to mix to a pouring consistency. Stir over a low heat until Copha has melted. Pour over cake and spread to the edges.

Honey Cake